BE

BE
By Dr. Carrie Jean Crawford

BE
Copyright © 2024 by Bishop Dr. Carrie J. Crawford

Requests for information should be addressed to:

KJH Ministries Publishing House
P.O. Box 97 Beaumont, MS 39423

ISBN: 979-8-218-37188-3

All scripture quotations unless otherwise noted, are taken from The Holy Bible-King James Version

All rights reserved. This book or any portion thereof may not be reproduced or used in any manner whatsoever without the express written permission of the publisher except for the use of brief quotations in a book review.

Cover designed by Professional Style Printing

Printed in the United States of America

First Printing, 2024

Bishop Carrie J. Crawford
294 John Thompson Rd.
Richton, MS 39476

bishopcrawford1953@gmail.com

TABLE OF CONTENTS

Foreword..
BE.. 1
Faith Over Fear.................................... 4
King's Kids.. 5
Hope... 7
Greater.. 9
Overcomers.. 11
Through... 13
I Can... 15
Right Hand.. 16
Declaring... 18
Perfect Peace..................................... 20
Trust... 21
Comfort... 23
Joy Comes... 25
Psalms 23... 27
Requests.. 28
Rejoice... 30
Pray.. 31
Good Fight.. 33
Sacrifice Of Praise............................... 35
Exalt God... 37
A Keeper.. 39
His Face.. 41
The Reward.. 43
The Rewarder...................................... 45
My Trust.. 47
He Answers.. 49
God Is Good....................................... 50
Renew... 52
Walking In Faith.................................. 54
Wisdom.. 56
Profit.. 58

FOREWORD

Bishop Carrie Jean Crawford has been a crucial partner in the spreading the Gospel of Jesus Christ. She's not only a trusted confidante but has also played roles similar to those of a daughter, mother, and steadfast friend for many years. This is a testament to the extraordinary character bestowed upon her by divine providence. Personally, I attribute much of my own success to the sagacious counsel she has provided on numerous occasions. Without her timely and profound insights, I am certain my present standing would assuredly be markedly different.

Bishop Crawford's ministry has brought transformative power to a multitude of individuals. From the least to the greatest, she continues to share the grace of God with all who cross her path. Bishop Crawford is unmistakably positioned within the Kingdom for a purposeful time like this.

One might wonder, "What credentials qualify Bishop Crawford to write this exceptional literary work?" The answer lies unequivocally in the narrative of her challenging journey, a journey that inherently attests to her qualifications. Bishop Carrie Crawford's path in ministry and life is marked by triumph over considerable challenges. As a female preacher/bishop navigating the ecclesiastical landscape of the South, she has faced criticism, overcome obstacles, and weathered rejection from diverse quarters. Bishop Crawford is no stranger to personal tragedies, including the loss of a child to a tragic accident and a courageous battle with the formidable adversary of cancer. In the face of these trials, she not only emerged victorious but presently stands as a resilient figure in the Body of Christ.

For those grappling with the challenge of placing one foot in front of the other, the time has come to receive the profound insights of an overcomer and, thereby, discover the fortitude to exist in fullness. This literary composition by Bishop Crawford will encourage, reenergize and revitalize any believer experiencing the existential struggle to 'BE.'

Bishop Kevin J. Hollingsworth

BE

I shall not die, but live, and declare the works of the Lord.
(Psalms 118:17)

This devotional is dedicated primarily to those who have faced the challenges of cancer and to those currently in the midst of this battle. It also serves as an uplifting message for anyone in need of encouragement.

This is my testimony. In November 2009, I discovered an unusual lump on my left side in the underarm area of my breast. Initially, I dismissed it, thinking it might be a result of a minor injury. Perhaps it was nothing. The initial response is often denial. Why is it that, among all diseases, the mere mention of cancer invokes the most fear?

Personally, up until that moment when I first felt the lump and realized it was not normal, the fear of cancer began to creep in. Finally, after two weeks of observation with no disappearance of the lump, I knew it was time to seek professional medical advice.

Following denial, the "what ifs" set in. As I sat in the doctor's office waiting, the spirit of fear attempted to erode away at my faith and determination to trust the Lord, whom I had accepted as my Savior.

Perhaps it's important to pause here and acknowledge those of you who haven't made that decision yet but are reading this devotional. I pray that, by the time you finish reading these scriptures and words of encouragement, you'll at least contemplate where you'll spend eternity. If you don't believe in a higher power or God, my prayer is that these words on paper will motivate you to undertake a soul search.

Now, back to my story. By the time my doctor entered the room, I had reflected on my life and taken inventory. Fear whispered that if it was cancer, I would succumb like everyone else. However, God had placed a personal witness in my life early on. I had seen her survive and be victorious for over 15 years. Still, this didn't fully convince me. I knew that cancer takes a different face for each person. I resolved to rise above the spirit of fear.

When I told the doctor why I was there, he immediately went into high gear. Looking me in the eye, he said, "I'm sending you for another mammogram, biopsy, and x-ray." Despite having had a mammogram a few months prior, his urgency allowed me to complete all the necessary tests that day.

Now came the wait — the challenging period before receiving the test results. During that time, it feels like you're waiting forever. The results confirmed cancer in my left breast, and I was scheduled to see an oncologist. I didn't even know the first thing about oncologists. I began to pray; my prayer was, "Lord, I want the best one." God answered but not as I expected. He said, "No, pray that you can be a witness, and I'll take care of the rest." I can testify that's exactly what He did.

The choice of surgeons and the decision to have a lumpectomy or mastectomy were unfamiliar terms to me. But one thing I knew: God was with me. Whatever was to be would be. I had an assurance that, no matter where this road led me, I was not alone. I opted for a mastectomy, and the course of treatment included chemotherapy and radiation. The cancer had already invaded my lymph nodes. Despite it being stage 3 and involving the lymph nodes, my oncologist was aggressively optimistic about my diagnosis and recovery.

Here I am, twelve years later, finally penning this devotional to encourage you. Admittedly, the assignment was given to me earlier, and I ask the Lord to forgive my procrastination. My prayer now is that it serves as encouragement to you on your journey.

My message to you is simple: live to BE.

Faith Over Fear

For God hath not given us the Spirit of fear, but of power, and of love and of a sound mind. 2nd Timothy 1:7

We are fortunate to contemplate the abundant gifts bestowed upon us by God: love, a sound mind, and power. Reflecting on John 3:16, we are reminded of the profound love God has for the world, demonstrated by the sacrifice of His only begotten Son. Those who believe in Him are promised eternal life.

In moments when the spirit of fear attempts to infiltrate my thoughts, bringing with it negative feedback and eroding my mind, I find solace in the knowledge that such fear does not come from God. The triumphant formula lies in choosing faith over fear, embracing a sound mind empowered by love to overcome any adversity.

God's desire is for us to place our trust in Him and His Word. The enemy seeks to kill, steal, and destroy, but Jesus came to offer us abundant life. When your mind faces assault from the adversary, remember that we are not victims but victors. It is crucial to declare the Word of God and meditate on it. Weed out any thoughts that hinder your victory. Speak life! Speak victory! Proclaim it with such strength that you can hear yourself declaring your triumph.

DECLARE IT LOUD! Embrace the power of God's Word and let it resonate within you, affirming your victory over fear and the schemes of the enemy.

King's Kids

Now faith is the substance of things hoped for, the evidence of things not seen. (Hebrews 11:1)

As a believer, I've been endowed with a measure of faith, a gift that grows as I immerse myself in the Word of God. Faith, as the scriptures declare, comes by hearing His Word. To overcome any challenge, belief is essential – a belief that James underscores must be demonstrated through actions, not merely words.

My hope is anchored in the actions that substantiate my faith. The Word of God prompts me to trust in the unseen, recognizing the power of life and death in the spoken word. I can speak into existence those things that are not as though they already are. Whether it's healing, deliverance, or any need, the key is to believe, declare, and activate your faith. Coming to God requires a fundamental belief that He exists and rewards those who earnestly seek Him. Believe!

God's concern extends to every facet of our lives. Let your faith be operational. Our battle is not against flesh and blood, and our weapons are not of the earthly realm. Victory is achieved through the power of the Word of God and the strength of our faith.

By donning the complete armor outlined in Ephesians Chapter 6, we fortify ourselves against spiritual opposition. Having equipped ourselves, we can withstand challenges and, having done all, stand firm. Can you see the picture? We are children of the Most High, God is our King. He sent His

Son to redeem us from the clutches of the enemy. We are royalty, children of the King. Defeat is not our destiny; we stand victorious.

HOPE

May the God of hope fill you with all joy and peace in believing, so that by the power of the Holy Spirit you may abound in hope. (Romans 15:13)

In the face of life's trials, there are moments when it feels like we might be overwhelmed. Yet, I am grateful for my God, who is my source of hope. His Word assures me that if I keep my mind steadfast on Him, He will grant me peace. Let the encouragement found in His Word and the trust we place in Scripture be our guiding light. Trials will come, but let us not be dismayed, for hope is our anchor, and the joy of the Lord is our strength.

Our Lord and Savior, Jesus, came to show us the way to overcome. All power has been given unto Him, and as the "Sons of God," we inherit His promises. We are a royal priesthood, born again by the blood of Jesus Christ, and hope is a significant part of our inheritance. Scripture even refers to Him as the God of Hope, a revelation that fills me with joy.

Faint not, for as you read, God is filling you with hope. Though we may experience weeping for a night, joy comes in the morning. My hope rests in the God who spoke all things into existence by His Word. Look up, for He offers us Power Everlasting. When I feel lost, I channel my thoughts and meditate on the One who promises, "I will never leave you, nor forsake you." I look to the hills, for my help comes from God.

Prayer is a powerful force. With the assurance and surety that hope provides, I can believe God for all things. Hope is a divine gift bestowed upon us by God. "For I know the plans I have for you," declares the Lord, "plans to prosper you and not to harm you, plans to give you hope and a future" (Jeremiah 29:11).

My hope rests in the Deliverer, who delights in me because of His unfailing love. Keep hope alive, and you will make it through.

GREATER

Ye are of God, little children, and have overcome them: because greater is he that is in you, than he that is in the world. (1st John 4:4)

What an empowering message! Greater indeed means more than average, and God declares that you are more than average. Regardless of the challenges you face, simply believe in GREATER! GREATER than hardships, GREATER than sickness, even the daunting disease called cancer, which inspired the writing of this devotional.

God assures us that we have overcome. You have overcome and I have overcome. His Word instructs us to first believe that He is. I believe; what about you? If there's any trace of unbelief, simply say, "Lord, I believe; help my unbelief." This honest confession to the Father is enough. Focus not on unbelief or fear but on the God who declares that we have overcome.

Take a moment to look around you. Perhaps you see a room with a television and various pieces of furniture. Don't be distracted by what you see; put on your spiritual glasses. Now, what do you see? Let me paint a picture for you. Begin to bring your mind into alignment with the Spirit. How? Meditate on the Word, on Jesus. Fill your mind with His presence—play some worship music if needed. Worship helps relax your mind and brings you into His presence. Feel His greatness. There's a peace and calmness that takes over. Are you there yet? If not, keep trying. He inhabits the praise of His people, and true worship happens in Spirit and Truth.

God's greatness resides in us. His greatness makes us victorious. We are winners. No matter how you may feel, remember that He who is in us is greater than he who is in the world. No weapon formed against you shall prosper. Finally, repeat after me: GREATER!

OVERCOMERS

For whatever is born of God overcomes the world and this is the victory that overcomes the world, our faith.
(1st John 5:4)

What a powerful reminder of the transformative nature of faith and the concept of being born again. Jesus, in his conversation with Nicodemus, emphasized the need for a spiritual rebirth. Although Nicodemus questioned the possibility of physical rebirth, the essence lies in accepting Jesus as our Lord and Savior, leading to a spiritual rebirth where we overcome the world through our connection with God.

Success is often a journey with ups and downs, victories and setbacks. Despite the challenges, the key is to remain focused and steadfast in our faith in God. The lyrics "We fall down but we get up" echo the truth that, as righteous individuals, we may stumble but always rise again. Our status as over-comers is not determined by instantaneous success but by consistently aligning our mindset with God's Word.

The power of our thoughts cannot be understated. Our mindset can either be our greatest downfall or a source of strength. By understanding that we are over comers through the blood of the Lamb and our spoken testimony, we gain the strength to face trials with a mindset rooted in God. Trials are inevitable, but our mindset should already be anchored in God. He is faithful, and His promises are unwavering. When difficulties arise, remember that you have already been declared an overcomer. The adversary may attempt to accuse and devour, but our faith in God's declaration of victory overcomes any legal accusation.

Embrace the greater within you, the part that God has already declared to be an overcomer. You are more than a conqueror, and as the accuser roars, let your response echo the truth:

"Yes, I am an OVERCOMER!"

THROUGH

Through thee will we push down our enemies, through thy name will we tread them under that rise up against us.
(Psalm 44:5)

A beautiful testament to the power that God has bestowed upon us through the Holy Spirit. Indeed, the Holy Spirit serves as our keeper, comforter, and teacher, and it is through His indwelling presence that we find the power to achieve the seemingly impossible. As the temple of the Holy Spirit, we possess the divine authority to stand firm in our faith, resisting any attempts to deny or diminish it.

Commissioned with the power of God's Word, we can confidently tread upon serpents, drink any deadly thing, and remain unharmed. Jesus, by His death and resurrection, made it possible for the Holy Spirit to come and abide within us, providing us with the strength to push through challenges. Despite the difficulties we may face, our victory is assured because Jesus conquered death and the grave. We are more than conquerors; we are overcomers.

Paul's declaration to let nothing separate him from the love of Christ serves as a powerful reminder that it is our faith—not fear—that makes us overcomers. Our faith in the promises of God, including healing through the stripes of Jesus, triumphs over the circumstances we see and hear in the natural realm.

In moments of darkness, remember that weeping endures for a night, but joy comes in the morning. Jesus is the way, the truth, and the life. So, wait patiently, endure without growing weary, and trust that in due season, you will reap if you faint not. Keep your mind strong, recognizing that the battlefield of the mind requires nourishment with the Word for renewal, bringing healing, deliverance, and peace.

Through it all, cling to the name of Jesus, and you will emerge victorious—strong, renewed, and empowered.

Through!

I CAN

I can do all things through Christ which strengtheneth me. (Philippians 4:13)

"I can rejoice. I can pray. I can sing. I can see. I can receive my healing. I can bless because I am a blessing to be a blessing. I can walk in truth. What are your all things? Whatever it may be, Christ has made it possible to succeed.

If not for the grace of God, the spirit of fear would overtake us. When we survey and ponder things in our natural mind, we can be consumed by our emotions and thoughts. It is in this place where I learn not to lean on my understanding but to acknowledge God. He is bigger than and greater than any obstacles in my way. It is at this place my renewed mind and spiritual perception must supersede the natural or carnal mind. Scripture tells us to be carnally minded is death, but to be spiritually minded is life and peace (Romans 8:6).

Thus, I come to the place where I must trust Jesus and his Word. Trust means to me I put greater weight on the Word of God than what I may see or feel. Thy Word, oh Lord, have I hid in my heart that I might not sin against thee. Satan, our adversary, is an accuser of the brethren. When we feel weak or defeated, (Philippians 4:13) I can do all things through Christ who strengthens me. This verse is an encourager.

God wanted you and me to know that we are victors and not victims. My mental status is I can! This is the way I must view my outcome. Maybe I am not feeling it, but I must believe the Word of God. In times when it is hard to grab hold of truth, I have learned to meditate or just continue to think on His Word until I feel a breakthrough. With God, all things are possible. Amen."

RIGHT HAND

So do not fear, for I am with you; do not be dismayed, for I am your God. I will strengthen you and help you; I will uphold you with my righteous right hand. (Isaiah 41:10)

"There are times when, no matter how hard we try, fear will come creeping in through our backdoor. This is when I have to anchor down my mind and realize that emotions are real, but they don't have to control us. Emotions or feelings were given to us by God so that we could be human.

Unfortunately, a lot of times we rely on our emotions more than our spirit man. I must trust God to bring me to the realization of His Word and not my emotions. I learned that having faith in His word is my anchor. When feelings are loud and my emotions are hypersensitive, God's word must overrule my emotions and my feelings. If I am to be an overcomer, I know that I can't lean unto my understanding.

The promise unto me is, 'I will never leave you nor forsake you.' He is my strength. He will uphold me with His righteous right hand. Good news! Jesus, when I call, I know you will answer. Pain and sickness are not the end; Jesus is in all situations. He is Alpha and Omega, the beginning and the end. He keeps on strengthening me. His grace is sufficient. Jesus told Paul that when he asked for the thorn in his flesh to be removed. Even so, I claim His grace is sufficient in my life.

The right hand denotes power. The God we serve has all power. We fear when we allow our thoughts to override His power. God is our source of strength, and He is more than able to sustain us when we are overcome by our own feelings. He wants us to realize that we can depend on Him. In Him, we live, we move, and we have our being. Glory be to God, for He is our righteousness. He is the God that healeth thee.

Just think, our emotions, fear, depression, anxiety, hopelessness, and anything that we may experience in our bodies—God is the answer.

He is good, and He is more than enough."

DECLARING

But you are a chosen generation, a royal priesthood, an holy nation, a peculiar people, that ye should shew forth the praises of him who hath called you out of darkness into his marvelous light. (1st Peter 2:9)

"First, let us declare who we are—our identity in the Lord.

We are a chosen generation. He called and chose you and me; we are part of the chosen generation. We are not just any people; we are His people. Amazing, isn't it? Chosen means selected from something. What does this have to do with what I feel now? Everything! We are the sheep of His pasture. Let's say it, 'I am chosen.'

A royal priesthood. In Old Testament times, only if you were of the tribe of Levi could you become a priest. But now, when the veil was rent in the temple, when Jesus was resurrected, and the church was born, we who accept Him as our Lord and Savior are called a royal priesthood after the order of Jesus. Glory, hallelujah! Listen, we can come boldly to the throne of grace. No matter the situation, we have been chosen, and we are royalty—king's kids.

A holy nation. Not only are we chosen and royal, but we have been called to be holy. Wait, before you back up, I know what you may be thinking. Holy is not a denomination; it is a separation from and a commitment to. Jesus said, 'Be ye holy as I am holy.' Let me explain how I see it: He chose me, but I choose Him, to live a life pleasing to God. He declares me holy and righteous according to His life that He gave for me and the blood that He shed for me. Wow, what a holy exchange. For God so loved the world that He gave His only begotten Son, that whosoever believeth in Him should not perish but have everlasting life (John 3:16).

Look, not only have we been declared chosen, royal, and holy, but a peculiar people. I don't know about you, but in the worldly sense, I have felt peculiar all my life. When I read that scripture, suddenly a light was turned on for me. Revelation came. I am peculiar because He created me to be peculiar. Praise God, no longer bound but free to praise Him and give Him glory. Yes, He brought light and gave understanding and wisdom to those who seek it.

I declare His Word today. I am all that He has called me to be."

PERFECT PEACE

Thou wilt keep him in perfect peace, whose mind is stayed on thee; because he trusteth in thee. (Isaiah 26:3)

"Perfect peace, not just any peace, is what we all desire. In a world filled with chaos and disturbance, the power of it seems like a vacuum hose, aiming to suck us in like a vacuum cleaner. Sometimes, even our minds can be uneasy and disturbed. God has given us a promise: if we put our minds on Him, He will keep us in perfect peace.

Let's explore the word 'perfect' to gain a good understanding of that type of peace. 'Perfect' means being complete, full-grown, and in our intended place. So, God is saying not without flaws, but in harmony with Him—leaning not on our own understanding but acknowledging Him in all our ways. If peace is what we desire, God has given us the prescription for it. The hardest part seems to be consistency.

Distractions pull our minds away from God, distrust causes us to look for solutions in the wrong places, and we tend to follow our emotions instead of letting His Spirit lead us. But let us strive for that place in Him where peace abides. He is not the author of confusion; God desires us to rest in Him. When I seek that place and find it, I am in a state of contentment. I invite you there.

God is a comfort to my mind, body, and soul. Meditate, focus, and set your mind on things above. Determine not to be persuaded by what you see, but be at one with God and His Word. Peace is only obtained by a persistent focus on God. We must strive to keep our focus. He will keep us in perfect peace when we trust Him and cast all our cares on Him. Remember, peace and perfect love cast out all fear. Trust in God."

TRUST

Trust ye in the Lord forever, for in the Lord Jehovah is everlasting strength. (Isaiah 26:4)

"There are times when we find that our trust is waning. I am reminded that my trust compels me to look to my Savior. The Lord has never failed me, nor will He fail you. We must refuse to compare Him and His assurance to anything earthly; the Lord is not a man whose words cannot be trusted.

The Word of God is forever settled in heaven. What is settled in heaven shall be on earth. Our Father who art in heaven, Thy will be done on earth as it is in heaven. Trust God. He will never leave us; He has given us that promise. In Him, I can claim strength to face whatever may come my way.

We live in a world where there is much distrust because of misplaced confidence or even a lack of respect and accountability. Praise God, on Him, I can lean and depend, for He will never let me down.

Trust can be easily broken but much harder to mend. Jesus came so that we would not have to trust in man. He showed us the way; He bridged the gap between earth and heaven for us. Where man had failed, Jesus didn't; He went all the way to Calvary. Yes, it may seem strange to trust in someone you can't see, but believe, He is real. It is better to trust in the Lord than to put confidence in men (Psalms 118:8).

The Lord Jehovah is our strength. Trust is only attainable by what we believe to be true and dependable. God's Word is true and forever settled in heaven. Not one word, jot, or tittle, as the scripture says, shall pass until all is fulfilled. He sent His Word, and it shall not return void.

I can put my trust in His Word. His Word is my sustainer. There have been times when I grew weak along the way, but His Word has been my strength and my comforter. I can read it and gain strength, or I can hear it and it brings comfort to my spirit man, thus enlightening my total being. I encourage you to do the same. I believe that when you read these devotionals, you will be strengthened.

Trust God!"

COMFORT

Blessed be God, even the father of our Lord Jesus Christ, the Father of mercies, and the God of all comfort. Who comforteth us in all our tribulations, that we may be able to comfort them which are in trouble, by the comfort wherewith we ourselves are comforted. (2nd Cor. 1:3-5)

"In order to feel unafraid when we are in a time of darkness, read this scripture and then reread it until you know who your Comforter is. The Lord wants us to know that He is our comfort. If He is our comfort, then we can comfort others. As we give comfort, we receive comfort.

The Lord is able to keep and strengthen us even in our darkest moments. He sent the Holy Spirit to be our Comforter. He told His disciples that He must go away, but He would not leave them without comfort. Jesus said that the Holy Spirit would be our guide and lead us into all truth. Again, I say He is our Comforter. He can bring comfort to us no matter what we are facing. Just try Him and see how great a God we serve. Even right now, He knows and cares. As I write this and reflect on dark times in my life, God has been my Comfort and my Comforter. His love has overshadowed me so many times. I pray that even now, whether you are facing cancer, any sickness, or just going through, these words will bring encouragement to you.

I know my God is real. He has proven that to me time and time again. Oh, taste and see that the Lord is good. Comfort makes us feel secure. It can bring peace in the midst of a storm. He arose from the boat and spoke, "Peace, be still!"

The wind obeyed, and the storm ceased. I am talking about that same God.

Call on Him, and He will hear. Child of God, listen to His voice. Even if you are not a child of God, or should I say, you have not made Him your Lord, call, and He will guide you. I serve a big God and a loving God. He left the ninety-nine to go after the one. If you need comfort, He is there.

God went through Samaria to see the woman at the well. He wrote on the ground to spare the woman caught in the act of adultery. He found Peter to let him know he was still His disciple even though Peter had denied Him three times. He will not deny you comfort.

He is the God of the mountain as well as the God of the valley. His rod and His staff comfort me. They keep me in a safe place. He comforts us so that we, in return, may be able to offer comfort to someone else who may be going through tribulation. What He has given me, I give unto you.

Faith endures!"

JOY COMES

All you saints! Sing your hearts out! Thank him to his face! He gets angry once in a while but across a lifetime there is only love. The nights of crying your eyes out give way to laughter. (Psalms 30:5- Msg.)

Praise be to God, acknowledging that while we may endure weeping through the night, we find solace in the promise that joy will arrive in the morning. It is a comforting truth to know that joy is assured and will bring a rejuvenation to our spirits. The strength we gain emanates from the joy of the Lord.

The Scriptures guide us on how to attain joy. We are encouraged to leap for joy, transcending our tears and actively reaching for the joy that awaits us. Let us audaciously leap! Singing a new song unto the Lord, we open our mouths to let praises resound. Our offering is a sacrifice of praise, not in the form of a sheep or lamb, but through the fruit of our lips, which brings joy to God. In return, He bestows joy upon us. Praise Him, and when words fail, the Holy Spirit intercedes on our behalf, comprehending our needs.

Even in the depths of depression, oppression, and darkness, we are called to press forward and leap. Sing a new song to God, irrespective of the melody's perfection; what matters is singing from the heart. God perceives the intentions of our hearts, recognizing our highs and lows. Whether on the mountaintop or in the valley, we affirm that the Lord is our shepherd, and we lack nothing. God is sufficient.

Contemplating His goodness brings joy, and gratitude wells up for His boundless mercy. Each day is recognized as a God day, regardless of external conditions. Rainy and cloudy days are embraced with a declaration that all is well, for we have a GREAT GOD! Let's repeat the affirmation until we truly believe it.

Reflecting on God's goodness and past deeds initiates a joyful leap. Joy, as a source of strength, rejuvenates feeble bones. The soul becomes overwhelmed with gratitude for His healing, deliverance, strength, and joy.

Believe without doubt that joy is forthcoming. Though we may weep for a night, rest assured, joy will dawn.

Receive your JOY with unwavering faith!

Psalm 23

READ THIS OFTEN!

Psa 23:1 A Psalm of David. The LORD is my shepherd; I shall not want. 2 He maketh me to lie down in green pastures: he leadeth me beside the still waters. 3 He restoreth my soul: he leadeth me in the paths of righteousness for his name's sake. 4 Yea, though I walk through the valley of the shadow of death, I will fear no evil: for thou art with me; thy rod and thy staff they comfort me. 5 Thou preparest a table before me in the presence of mine enemies: thou anointest my head with oil; my cup runneth over. 6 Surely goodness and mercy shall follow me all the days of my life: and I will dwell in the house of the LORD for ever.

MY FAITH MANTRA!

REQUESTS

Be careful for nothing; but in everything by prayer and supplication with thanksgiving let your requests be made known unto God. (Philippians 4:6)

We often find ourselves burdened with requests, yet sometimes we fail to entrust them to the right person. Thankfully, God encourages us in His Word not to be anxious about anything. He desires that we refrain from worry and concern, urging us to cast all our cares upon Him because He cares for us individually. In the vastness of this world, it's truly remarkable that God can attend to every single one of our concerns.

Pride and shame can hinder us from sharing our troubles with God. The enemy often employs shame as a tool to keep us downtrodden and even depressed. However, there is nothing too challenging for God to handle. Are you ready to make your issues His issues? Let's do it—set aside pride and shame, inviting Jesus into every aspect of our lives.

Worry and anxiousness lead to stress, which can, in turn, impact our health and mental well-being. God has provided us with a solution: don't worry—give it to Him. Prayer and praise are powerful, winning combinations. Just as Paul and Silas prayed and sang in prison, seeing the doors open, you too can be set free from the prison of worries by making known your requests known to God.

God is the ultimate problem solver and peace maker. Entrust everything to Him and trust that He will make a way where there seems to be none. His grace is more than sufficient.

Regardless of how impossible it may seem with man, remember that with God, all things are possible. Trust Him, witness His miraculous work, and know that He is a good God. He wants us to have faith in Him and not be dismayed by our problems.

If you're already stressed, what do you have to lose? Try God for yourself, believe in His Word, and experience the truth that His Word is faithful. I speak to you now: give whatever concerns you to our heavenly Father, and He will lead you to a good outcome. Thanksgiving and prayer are the potent tools we can employ to defeat the enemy of our souls.

REJOICE!

Rejoice evermore. (1st Thess. 5:16)

Rejoicing goes beyond mere emotion; it's a profound expression of delight in our God. The fact that God sent His only begotten son for our redemption is a compelling reason for rejoicing. In moments of despair, when we feel lost, God provides a resting place and lifts us up. Rejoicing has become a way of life, surpassing any earthly reward.

While trials, problems, and sickness are part of life, God remains worthy of all praise. Regardless of our circumstances, He is our answer, a bridge over troubled waters, our healer, and deliverer. This testimony is an invitation for you to find your own place to rejoice, knowing that it transforms the mind, lifts the spirit, and has a positive impact on the body.

In times of pain, choosing to rejoice becomes a potent medicine. Even when we don't feel like it, deciding to rejoice and praise God is a powerful declaration. The psalmist's words ring true: "I will be filled with joy because of you. I will sing praises to your name, O Most High" (Psalm 9:2 NLT). This commitment to rejoice despite circumstances is an empowering declaration to overcome defeat. Join in praising and shouting unto the Lord, for He is truly good.

REJOICE!

PRAY!

Pray without ceasing. (1st Thess. 5:17)

"Just what is this scripture asking me to do: 'pray without ceasing'? How is that even possible? I will explain what works for me. First, it is a mindset. Second, this is an exercise that I have to consistently work at. The mind is always active; therefore, I set my mind on things of God whenever there is opposition to the will of God. I have learned to meditate on His Word even when I am working with my hands.

Now, I can't tell you how to pray because that is personal. Praying develops out of your relationship with God. Maybe you are just beginning to know Him. May I suggest that you begin by talking to Him just as you would a friend? I would like to share with you an experience I had a few years back with my sister. She was very sick, and because she was in a room where she could hear our father pray, she became intimidated by his praying method. She shared this with me, and I told her that prayer is simply communication between you and God. I said just talk to God like you're talking to me, and He hears and understands. Speak from your heart. I wish you could have seen the relief that came across her face. My father, over the years, had developed a form of communication with God that probably mirrored what he had been accustomed to hearing at that time. Whereas my sister was of another era, so she felt the way she was praying in comparison to my father was wrong. But God hears all His children; our methods may be different, but talking to Him is all that matters. I can't begin to imagine if my sister would have allowed the intimidation of my father's praying to stop her from praying for herself. I shared that experience so that you would know the enemy will use whatever he can to distract you. Don't be distracted.

Pray often. Have a mindset to pray even when the winds are blowing against you. Prayer opens up avenues for God to come in and do mighty things. Be anxious for nothing, but in all things, with thanksgiving and prayer and supplication, make your request known to God. Jesus stole away to pray to the Father often, as we have to continue in prayer, knowing and believing that God hears us. As you grow in prayer, you find that it can bring you peace and put you in a place of rest. Prayer doesn't have length or time. Anytime, anyplace, no matter how long or how short, always give space to pray.

Pray without ceasing and watch God work on your behalf. Just communicate with Him; He is waiting to hear from you.

PRAY!

GOOD FIGHT!

Fight the good fight of faith, lay hold unto eternal life, where unto thou art also called, and hast professed good profession before many witnesses. (Timothy 6:12)

You may be asking, now what is a good fight? A "good fight" in this context involves maintaining consistency, perseverance, and an unwavering determination to keep pressing forward without giving in to defeat. In the natural sense, it's comparable to enduring rounds in a boxing match and refusing to stay down. Our victory lies not in our own strength but in God, in whom we live, move, and have our being. Jesus has already secured the ultimate triumph, and we fight from a standpoint of victory. The encouragement is to fight the good fight without succumbing to the option of quitting.

Confession becomes a powerful weapon as we proclaim our victory and declare ourselves as victors, not victims, in Christ Jesus. Despite the enemy's whispers of defeat, we must resist the voice of negativity. God, our captain, is a winner, and the race is given to those who endure to the end. In moments when quitting seems tempting, we hold onto God's unchanging hand. When we've done all to stand, we stand firm.

It's crucial not to give up. Seeking strength from God, who is our keeper, our Alpha and Omega, the author, and finisher of our faith, is a key strategy. Jehovah Rophe, our healer, sustains us when we are weak. Prayer, meditation, and calling upon the name of the Lord bring assurance that He hears and answers in His perfect timing.

Fighting is synonymous with refusing to give up because we already know that God is on our side. Staying in the race ensures we can't lose, with a cloud of witnesses cheering us on. Called and chosen, it is indeed a good fight of faith.

Faith, the force that moves mountains, motivates us to trust in Jesus, who will not let us down, leave us, or forsake us. With confidence in the Almighty God, we are persuaded to fight the good fight. If you're reading this devotion, you are encouraged to join in the victorious journey. Rise up, let's move forward; witnesses are watching, believing that we can make it.

Fight the good fight of faith!

SACRIFICE OF PRAISE

By him therefore let us offer the sacrifice of praise to God continually, that is the fruit of our lips giving thanks to his name. (Hebrews 13:15)

Listen, may the words of my mouth and the meditation of my heart be pleasing in Your sight, O Lord, my Rock, and my Redeemer. When we consider praise, it's often associated with a sound. I appreciate what the elders used to say — sometimes you just have to moan. There were instances when I lacked words, and a simple moan would well up from my heart to my lips. I began this devotion with that particular scripture to seek coverage in those dark moments. It's during those times when my spoken words and my heart's reflections may seem at odds with God's Word. Even when I desire to praise Him in my spirit, my flesh might protest. In the presence of pain or doubt, praising a God who allows such challenges becomes a difficult task. Yet, we are instructed to offer the sacrifice of praise. In these moments, my praise truly becomes a sacrifice. My lips would often prefer to complain than to give praise.

Praise be to God! I thank Him because He understands my heart. Deep within, I am conscious of His goodness even while traversing through fiery trials. In my heart, I recognize that He won't burden me beyond what I can endure. I am aware that He is working for my ultimate good. So, I express my gratitude, adoration, and praise for what He is doing within me, even as I endure fiery trials. I offer the sacrifice of praise with my mouth to convey my thankfulness to Him. Are you following me? This has a personal touch because it was challenging during moments of physical pain.

I make this declaration to affirm that it can be done. I did it, and so can you. Let's simply say, HALLELUJAH! Did you know "HALLELUJAH" is the highest word of praise? Say it again, "HALLELUJAH!" You've just praised Him. If that's all the praise you can utter at this time, just say that. Soon, more words will follow. "HALLELUJAH."

It's astonishing how the power of the Holy Spirit will begin to speak through you. I have been profoundly moved by the power working through me to offer God praise at my weakest moments. He is a faithful God. He is a miracle-working God. He knows our hearts even when we don't fully understand them ourselves. He can speak through us to bring about His will if we submit to Him. The Bible says, submit to God, resist the devil, and he will flee. Every time the enemy tries to fill your mind with negative thoughts or doubts, remember that praise will drive the devil away.

Let's try it again, **"HALELUJAH!"**

EXALT GOD

O Lord, thou art God; I will exalt thee, I will praise thy name; for thou hast done wonderful things; thy counsels of old are faithfulness and truth. (Isaiah 25:1)

How I cherish His Word! God's Word has become my foundation, a solid rock in my life. This scripture resonates deeply with me. The "I will" signifies my commitment to declare what I am eager to do. Often, I find myself rushing through life, overlooking the very things that have sustained and guided me through the darkest valleys. But I will exalt Him; I will praise Him because I intimately know what He has done for me. Looking back and witnessing where He has brought me from compels me to affirm, "I will."

This is the day that the Lord has made, and I will be glad and rejoice in it. I will declare that He is my Lord and my strength. I will raise the praises of His name. I will sing a new song unto the Lord. I will exalt His name forever, for He is a magnificent God. I will encourage you to "taste and see that the Lord, He is good." I will enter His gates with thanksgiving and His courts with praise.

Exaltation creates an atmosphere for my God to come and dwell. It shifts me out of the center and places God on the throne of my heart. As the song says, if a robin can say thank you, then so can I. It becomes easy when we recognize that He is the reason we exist. He sacrificed His life to save ours.

The Bible declares that without the shedding of blood, there is no remission of sins. Glory be to God Almighty, for He sent His Son, Jesus, who shed His sinless blood for us. He was the perfect lamb, the unblemished sacrifice, and He died for you and me. That is one significant reason why I will exalt and praise Him. To name a few more reasons; He is my healer. He is my peacekeeper. He is the wheel in the middle of the wheel. He is the author and finisher of my faith. He is my redeemer. I could continue, but you're starting to grasp the picture. The "why" and the "how" are rooted in the fact that He is the great I Am.

One of the most profound feelings I've experienced is being in His presence. Words cannot fully describe it. I invite you to try it for yourself. My God is real. I may not see Him, but I certainly can feel Him, and oh, what an experience it is. Try Jesus and feel His love envelop you as He lifts you into heavenly places. Joy unspeakable and blessings beyond measure await all who allow Him to come in.

O Lord, You are God. Yes, He is the mighty God. God is our comfort in times like these. When I exalt Him, I am simply saying, "Lord, I trust You. Your faithfulness and truth have surpassed time. I thank You for all You have done."

A KEEPER

But the Lord is faithful, who shall stablish you, and keep you. (2nd Thess.3:3).

This Word is undeniably powerful. The need to feel kept is universal, a desire for assurance and security that transcends our perceived independence. To be free from worry about the intricacies of life is indeed a grand aspiration. Even as women, despite our sense of independence, there remains a fundamental need to feel kept. The Lord, in His faithfulness, is the constant presence that never wavers, always there, no matter the circumstances. I've come to realize the importance of placing my trust in God, even before the diagnosis of cancer.

Fear often attempts to overtake the mind, with persistent "what ifs" and "how comes" nagging in the background. This is the crucial moment when I must declare the Word of God. The Lord is faithful. In the darkest nights, when my body is weak and my mind is tormented, He has pulled me through. As the song beautifully expresses, "He was there all the time, waiting patiently in line," waiting for me to believe and take Him at His Word.

Evil, in its various forms, is an ever-present force seeking to steal, kill, and destroy. Yet, God will keep me. God will keep you. He establishes us in His Word, for He is the Word. All we need to do is believe.

The psalmist's words echo the truth: "Trust in the Lord, lean not unto your own understanding, and He will direct your paths." He is faithful and true, never once breaking His promises. It all boils down to faith and confidence in Him. He came that we might have life and have it more abundantly. Living in Him, depending on Him, and forsaking what we see, we can rest assured that God is our eternal keeper.

A keeper, yes He is!

HIS FACE

For the eyes of the Lord are over the righteous, and ears are open unto their prayers but the face of the Lord is against them that do evil. (1st Peter 3:12)

I am often reminded of a scripture found in the Bible, God's Holy Word. This devotional aims to uplift and encourage our spirits, finding assurance and strength in the sacred text. If it weren't for the truth and faith in God's Word, I doubt I would be sharing this devotional. One scripture says, "The Lord make his face to shine upon thee and be gracious unto thee" (Numbers 6:25), while another encourages us to "Look to the Lord and his strength, seek his face always" (Psalm 105:4). These verses provide me with assurance and peace.

There are times when we question whether God cares and why we are going through certain challenges. Allow me to encourage you by affirming that He does care, and He knows. Even in our moments of weakness, we find strength in Him. It is essential to resist trusting the doubtful voices in our heads and, instead, to believe in God. We must trust Him. He is good and faithful. To overcome challenges, His Word must be our source of strength and our protector.

When we pray and seek His face, He attentively hears our cries. I can vouch for the fact that I have tried Him, and He has never failed me. I emphasize again, He is faithful. God is my refuge and strength, and I can depend on Him for everything. He is not merely a healer but the great I Am. Whatever you need, now and forever, just call on Him. I am grateful that He never gave up on me, and I am confident that He never will. Though I may have given up on myself at times, He was there every time to lift me back up.

Prayer is a potent weapon at our disposal in all situations. It builds faith and doesn't need to be lengthy; sincerity from the heart matters most. He sees and hears the cries of His children.

Abba Father!

THE REWARD

Cast not away therefore your confidence, which hath great recompense of reward. (Hebrews 10:35)

Certainly, everyone appreciates being rewarded, often seen as a symbol of achievement. The book of Hebrews emphasizes that when we approach God, our first belief should be that He exists and is a rewarder of those who diligently seek Him.

If you're reading this devotional, it implies you already hold a belief, and I would recommend considering placing your belief in God. Personally, I've found countless reasons to believe in God, having tried and experienced His faithfulness in my life. He is my healer, strength, comforter, peace, deliverer, and much more. The rewards of seeking Him are immeasurable, and when we seek Him for everything, He never fails.

Confidence in God is comparable, if not superior, to having money in the bank. While a bank's stability depends on backing, God needs no such assurance as He is the source of all. His Word is eternal and unwavering, providing a foundation that stands throughout eternity.

The scripture assures us that while weeping may endure for a night, joy will undoubtedly come in the morning. The distinction between "will" and "may" is crucial. Confidence, defined as faith or belief in someone's ability to act rightly and effectively, is the state of being certain. Our confidence in God's ability to keep or deliver us will be rewarded through our unwavering faith in Him.

The nature of the reward is often determined by the rewarder, and thankfully, God has made His rewards known in His Word. The requirements and how to receive these rewards are laid out clearly. Seeking Him first and His righteousness is the key, and everything else will be added unto us.

Be confident in God, for He is faithful to His Word. Endure with the assurance that God will reward your confidence in Him.

Trust him!

THE REWARDER

But without faith it is impossible to please him: for he that cometh to God must believe that he is and that he is a rewarder of them that diligently seek him. (Hebrew 11:6)

Absolutely, God is indeed a rewarder, and He responds to our faith. Throughout the Bible, those who approached Him received answers in accordance with their faith, as exemplified by Jesus' words: "Be it done unto you according to your faith." Today, as we bring our needs before Him, we can be assured that He will reward us accordingly.

God's faithfulness, justice, and mercy are unparalleled. He not only rewards but is a great rewarder, especially to those who diligently seek Him. From the outset, God intended to be our Lord, even granting humanity the choice to worship Him. Choosing to seek God and align our will with His is a pivotal aspect of our relationship with Him.

Worship is an acknowledgment of God's supreme nature. It is a recognition that He is the creator of all things. God desires worship that emanates from a sincere spirit and truth. True worship has the power to shift atmospheres and liberate us even in our lowest moments. God rewards those who worship Him for who He is, not merely for what He can provide. It's essential to seek God's face before seeking His hand.

The life of the Apostle Paul serves as a remarkable example. Formerly known as Saul, he actively opposed followers of Jesus. However, his encounter with Jesus on the road to Damascus transformed him, and he became a powerful apostle. Despite facing numerous challenges, Paul remained an unwavering worshiper, teaching us to persist in our connection with God. Even when confronted with a thorn in the flesh, he learned that God's grace was sufficient.

God's promises are trustworthy and He fulfills them consistently. Healing, peace, and eternal life are among the rewards for those who believe in Him. He is a great rewarder, responding to our faith and devotion with His unending grace and blessings.

MY TRUST

I will say of the Lord, he is my refuge and my fortress my God in him will I trust. (Psalm 91:2)

Absolutely, speaking the Word, proclaiming, and decreeing our faith and confidence in God is a powerful practice. Trusting in Him and relying on His Word provides a solid foundation that never wavers. It's a testament to His faithfulness and a source of strength, especially during challenging times.

When faced with uncertainties and storms of life, God becomes our refuge—a safe place to hide until the storms pass over. His Word is a constant and unwavering source of strength, even when our own faith might waver. Trusting in Him is not just a choice; it becomes a life source that sustains us.

God is our fortified place, undefeated and greater than any challenge life may bring. In Him, we find victory over sickness, adversity, and every trial we encounter. Calling upon the name of Jesus is a powerful declaration of our trust in the One who has overcome all things.

"I will say He is my refuge and my strength; in Him, will I trust." These words resonate with the assurance that, regardless of confusion, heartbreak, or betrayal, God remains a dependable refuge. Trusting in Him is not about what we see but about what He has already faced and conquered. To those who may feel broken and find it hard to trust again, the encouragement is not to give up. Determine in your mind that you are an overcomer. Trust in God, for His Word is trustworthy, solid, and enduring. Life and death are in the power of our tongue, and having faith in Him, believing He is, brings about great reward.

So, close your eyes, open your mouth, and declare, "Lord, I trust You. Regardless of what it looks like, I trust You. I believe, but Lord, help my unbelief." Be filled with expectation, for in trusting God, there is nothing to lose and everything to gain.

HE ANSWERS

In the day of trouble I will call upon thee: for thou wilt answer me. (Psalm 86:7)

Absolutely, there are moments in our lives when adversity strikes, and we yearn for someone to hear our cries. In those times, the psalmist provides us with a profound answer: "In the day of my trouble, I will call upon God, for He can hear and answer my call." What a reassuring truth to hold onto. God not only promises to answer but assures us of His constant presence, regardless of the challenges we face. When trouble arises, our first instinct should be to cry out to our heavenly Father, patiently awaiting His response, healing, deliverance, and comfort.

Trusting God with every concern is key, for He is unfailingly faithful. Unlike friends who may be occupied or unavailable at times, God is never too busy to answer our calls. Impatience may set in, but rest assured, God always comes through. He is a responsive and attentive God.

Fear, however, can be an enemy to our faith. It has the power to immobilize us, convincing us that nobody cares and that our cries will go unanswered. Yet, God can hear even the faintest cry, and He is genuinely concerned about us. Rise above fear and let faith prevail. God is our strength, the great "I am that I am." Whatever role you need Him to play in your life, He is more than capable. Choose faith over fear.

Calling upon His name is a powerful act, and God will answer. Trouble holds no weight when a child of God is in distress. Be assured, He will answer your call.

GOD IS GOOD

For the LORD God is a sun and a shield: the Lord will give grace and glory: no good thing will he withhold from them that will walk uprightly. (Psalm 84:11)

We can find comfort in knowing that God is both a source of warmth, like the sun, and a protector, like a shield. Reading this verse took me back to my childhood, living in a house where the only source of heat was a fireplace. The nights were cold when the fire died, and my granny would heat a smoothing iron to place at our feet for warmth. Memories of those days are bittersweet, but in God, the One I serve, I find both warmth and protection. What a mighty God we serve. These words bring great comfort to my mind, body, and soul.

God assures me that He will not withhold any good thing from me as long as I walk uprightly before Him. So, I commit to maintaining right standing, acknowledging all my ways unto Him and hiding His Word in my heart. If you are new at this, that's okay too—just trust Him. He will not leave you alone. He answers when we call, and He is a God of mercy and grace when we seek His face.

The comfort of knowing that God is my shield leads me to one of my favorite Psalms,

Psalms 91:1-2: *"He that dwelleth in the secret place of the most High shall abide under the shadow of the Almighty. I will say of the Lord, He is my refuge and my fortress: in Him will I trust."*

God is my sun and shield, and no good thing will He withhold from me. This promise extends to you—yes, you. With God, all things are possible, and my faith is anchored in Him. I can assure you that He is not only good but also faithful. Even when facing pain, like Job, we can declare, 'Though He slays me, yet will I trust Him.' I invite you to put your confidence and faith in Him. Everything around us may fail, but God never will; He will never forsake us. I make bold statements because I believe in God.

Why? Because God keeps His Word."

RENEW

"But they that wait upon the Lord shall renew their strength; they shall mount up with wings as eagles; they shall run and not be weary; they shall walk and not faint." (Isaiah 40:31)

Renew: *to increase the life of or replace something old; to begin doing something again.*

They that wait on the Lord can expect great things from God. Waiting is not a passive act, as we have somehow been made to think. Yes, we may have to wait in line or wait for the arrival of something. Even so, while we are waiting, we are engaged in some form of activity, if nothing but in our minds. These days there are so many things we can do even while we wait.

Sickness or any type of negativity in our bodies can bring us down. Let's talk about sickness, for instance, and cancer to be precise. When I began treatment, after the 2nd dose of chemotherapy, my body began to feel like it had been invaded by another being. Not only was my body under attack, but also my mind. Now I credit myself to be strong-minded; however, chemo seemed to be more persuasive than my mind and body. My body and mind were both in agreement that I would not survive these treatments. I was in a battle both physically and spiritually. Physically because the reality was my body and mind were going through something that I had never experienced before. I have always been able to speak to my mind and somewhat bring it into subjection. Spiritually, I am glad to have a personal relationship with God. I also am thankful to have friends who believed in the power of prayer and God's ability to heal. Really, to be truthful, this is the reason for the devotional: to encourage and lift up the spirit of those who may be facing cancer or any other trial of life.

The fact is, God was my strength. God was whom I called when I felt I was drowning and going down for the count. The times I felt that I would not take another dose, it was just too much to rebound from. But God never allowed me to wallow long in self-pity. He always came through. It is true that they that wait upon the Lord, their strength is renewed. God gives us whatever we need to rise above the storm. Yes, he renews our mind; he restores strength and determination to our body and mind. He renews us to get up and fight again.

Wait on the Lord! He will renew and ensure that we are able to continue the journey.

WALKING IN FAITH

Therefore we are always confident knowing that, whilst we are at home in the body, we are absent from the Lord; for we walk by faith, not by sight. (Galatians 5: 5-6)

Sometimes the path becomes dark, and our journey seems distorted. In those moments, we must continue to walk and exercise our faith in the One who sees all. Jesus is the way, the truth, and the life.

His Word serves as a light unto our path and a lamp unto our feet. Understanding that, no matter how dark it may seem in our lives, Jesus is the light. He declared, 'I am the light of the world. Whoever follows me will never walk in darkness but will have the light of life' (John 8:12).

Trusting in our flesh is futile because the flesh is weak. In Him, we live, move, and have our being. Walking by faith requires believing that God is everything in His Word. Faith is not merely about 'name it and claim it'; it's about believing in His Word, knowing that He is not a liar and does not bear false evidence. Our flesh is subject to failure due to the human condition, traced back to Adam and Eve's downfall in the garden. The good news is that God sent His Son to redeem us.

Paul comprehended the concept of being in the body but walking in the Spirit. Jesus is the conqueror who overcame death for us. While we desire a long life, our confidence should be in the Creator, not in what we see.

Our strength, healing, and deliverance are in Him. Salvation is in Him: 'For God so loved the world that He gave His only begotten Son, that whosoever believeth in Him should not perish but have everlasting life' (John 3:16).

Place yourself in God's hands, take Him at His Word, and let His Word become medicine for whatever ails you. He is the divine healer. Our bodies, this flesh, are corruptible, but when we align ourselves with God, whether we live or die, He is incorruptible, and we have passed from death unto life.

He lives, and because He lives, we live also in Him. **Just have faith, not in ourselves but in Him.**

Walk by faith! Walk in faith! Walk in the Spirit!

WISDOM

The fear of the Lord is the beginning of wisdom and the knowledge of the Holy is understanding. (Proverbs 9:10).

"There is a good and healthy fear that stems from understanding who God is. Recognizing that God possesses all power is the foundation of the trust He asks of us. He desires our trust and fear to be directed towards Him rather than towards man. Natural fear often contains elements of doubt and unbelief, while a healthy and spiritual awareness of God is considered wisdom. It involves acknowledging that, regardless of the fears we may allow ourselves to experience in the natural realm, God is greater than those fears. The fear of the Lord prolongs our ways, and the law of the wise is a fountain of life, steering us away from the snares of death. True wisdom lies in recognizing that everything begins and ends with our God — the Alpha and Omega, the beginning, and the end, the author, and the finisher of our faith.

Wisdom manifests as the ability to discern, exercise good judgment, and make decisions grounded in soundness, prudence, and intelligence. It involves hiding the Word of God in our hearts to guard against sin. Trusting our creator is a key component of wisdom, enabling us to overcome the fears of this world by relying on the fear of the Lord as our strength and source.

Wisdom actively seeks wise counsel and does not depend solely on its own strength but on the knowledge that God, who is above and all-knowing, is in control. Wisdom seeks to preserve us in Him. Trusting wisdom allows the fear of the

Lord to be our keeper, and understanding is granted to all who seek after Him. Often, reasoning aligns with our minds.

Knowledge is the ability to retain information obtained. While knowledge encompasses a wide range of information, for any, knowing God is of utmost importance. Understanding that God cares brings comfort to the very core of our being. This assurance is not meant to be kept to oneself but shared to bring comfort to others. Rest assured that God is no respecter of persons; He desires to provide the same comfort to all. Trust wisdom, let the fear of the Lord be your keeper, and understanding will be given to all who seek after Him."

PROFIT

For what shall it profit a man if he shall gain the whole world and lose his own soul? (Mark 8:36)

This is why I emphasize the need not to put confidence in the flesh. Our ultimate goal is to attain eternal life. Death is an enemy, but through Christ and living in Him, we find eternal life. Throughout this devotional, my aim has been to be an encourager and to point you to Christ. However, when everything is said and done, none of this matters if we don't personally know Him.

My prayer is that, by the end of this devotional, you will have received enough of the Word not only to be encouraged but also to have accepted the Lord as your Savior if that is the case. Salvation is our ultimate goal. Whether we are healed from cancer or face any other challenge, please feel and know that God is our only hope. The first step is to believe. Even in my weakest hour, as a believer, my faith was tested. The adversary can present a strong case.

In life, we face situations that require us to trust in something or someone. We can trust the doctor, a friend, a lawyer, a higher being, but there is no being higher than God. I choose to trust in God, and I pray you do too. God is, God was, and God will always be.

Whatever you need is in Him. Just in case you still have doubt, I say this: try Jesus. What have you got to lose? Even if you gain the whole world and everything you desire, you will still have lost it when you leave this side of the grave. However, the eternal life gained from trusting in God can be carried to the other side.

My friend, this is why I choose Christ as my Savior. He is all I need for renewal, salvation, healing, and continuous strength. He is all you need as well. God is interested in your well-being.

Profit or loss?

Made in the USA
Columbia, SC
23 September 2024